THROUGH THE PAIN

I0558983

A JOURNEY OF HEALING AND FAITH

Tina M

CONTENTS

INTRODUCTION: YOU ARE NOT ALONE

Pain and Depression are often silent. They don't always scream. Sometimes, they whisper in the quiet moments or sit beside us when no one else can see them. If you're holding this book, chances are you've felt that weight. Or maybe you're carrying it now.

This book was born from a place of truth. Not the kind wrapped in polished words or perfect ending, but the kind that aches, that lingers, and eventually, if you let it, heals.

I am not a doctor, nor do I claim to have all the answers. But I've walked through days that felt impossible, and I've learned that telling the truth about pain is the first step toward freedom. This book is not about fixing you – It's about seeing you. It's about honoring your journey, your scars, your silence.

Here, you'll find stories, reflection, and gentle truths. Some may feel heavy, but I promise – there is hope woven into every Chapter. You are not alone. And you never were.

CHAPTER 1:
THE FACES OF PAIN

Pain wears many faces. Some scream. Some smile. Some stay hidden behind makeup, laughter, or silence. It's not always visible, and that's what makes it so isolating.

Pain isn't just about physical wounds – it's about emotional loss, unspoken trauma, deep loneliness, and the battles we fight in the quiet of our minds. And Depression? It often walks hand in hand with pain. It dulls the light, steals the joy, and whispers lies that we are not enough.

What is Pain?

Pain Can be: Physical: Chronic Illness, Injury, Fatigue.

Emotional: Heartbreak, grief, betrayal.

Mental: Anxiety, intrusive thoughts, low self-worth.

Spiritual: Feeling lost, disconnected, or abandoned.

No Pain is "too small" or "not serious enough." If it hurts.

MY TRUTH:

I have been in pain for years. Some days, the pain felt like it swallowed me whole. It hasn't been easy – not for me, and not for my Family. But it was during those times, lying on my sick bed, that I began to truly see people for who they are. Pain reveals the kind of friends you have. Some walk away, some stay silent. But others – like Family and Children – stand by you – when you have nothing left to give.

If you have God and a Wonderful Family, be grateful. Their love is a lifeline. It was for me.

Understanding Depression:

Depression is not just sadness; it's a deep, unshakable numbness. You, my feel.

Tired all the time

Disconnected from people you love.

Like you're just "existing instead of living.

Empty, even when everything looks fine from the outside.

Depression can feel like drowning in slow motion. But recognizing it is the beginning of Healing.

WHY THIS CHAPTER MATTERS?

Before we move forward, we must name what we're dealing with. Pain loses some of its power when it's spoken aloud. Depression becomes less isolating when we say, This is real. I feel it. I'm not alone."

CHAPTER 2:
WHEN THE SILENCE FEELS LOUD

There's a kind of silence that isn't peaceful – it's heavy. It follows you from room to room, fills your mind with unanswered questions, and reminds you of everything you've lost or longed for. Pain and depression often speak the loudest when the world goes quiet.

The Loneliness No One Talks About:

You can be surrounded by people and still feel completely alone. That kind of loneliness makes you question your worth, your purpose, and sometimes even your will to keep going.

It's not that people don't care; it's that they often don't understand.

"Sometimes I wished someone.

Would just sit beside me and not try to fix me, just see me."

The Moments That Break You:

These moments come without warning. A smell, a song, a flash of memory – and suddenly, you're back in a place you've tried so hard to leave. These are the moments that test your strength.

But here's the thing: You survived that day. You're surviving this one, too.

Faith in the Dark:

When the silence grows too loud, faith becomes an anchor. Maybe you don't feel strong, but your faith doesn't need to be loud – it just needs to exist. Even a whisper to God, even a sigh that says, " Help", is enough.

"God doesn't always *change* our situation right away, but He leaves us in it alone."

It's Continues... When the Silence Feels Loud.

Coping in the Quiet:

When you're alone with your thoughts, it can feel like the darkness is closing in. But even in those quiet moments, there are gentle ways to cope and care for yourself:

- Write it out: Journaling can be like exhaling pain. You don't need to have the words, just honest ones.
- Talk to someone: Whether it's a friend, a family member, or a therapist, speaking your truth lightens the load.
- Breathe intentionally: Simple, breathe, slow, deep, and steady can bring calm in the middle of chaos.

- Lean of faith: Open your Bible, say a of prayer, or just sit in silence with God or sing a song of praise. He hears even the quietest cries.

You Are Not Invisible:

Even when it feels like no one notices your pain, you are seen. By God, by those who love you. And by others who are quietly fighting similar battles. This Chapter is for them too – for the strong ones who cry in secret, and for the ones who smile through suffering.

Final words from my Heart:

To anyone reading this: God is our Great Healer. I know what it feels like to be tired, to feel broken, to wonder if it will ever get better. But I'm here to tell you – don't give up. Life may not be easy, and the road may be long, but you are not walking it alone.

Even in silence, even in suffering, God is nearby. And healing, even if it comes slowly, is possible.

CHAPTER 3:
THE STRENGTH BEHIND THE SMILE

People often say, "You're so Strong." But they don't always see the tears behind closed doors, the silent prayers, or the night spent crying into a pillow. Strength doesn't always look like standing tall – it often looks like getting up again, even when everything hurts.

Smiling Through the Pain:

So many of us learn how to hide our pain:

- We smile so we don't have to explain.
- We say, " I'm fine," because we're afraid to be a burden.
- We laugh, even when our hearts are breaking, but behind that smile is a story. A struggle, A warrior. You.

Real Strength is Soft:

True strength isn't pretending everything is okay, it's allowing yourself to be Vulnerable. It's saying:

- "I need help."
- "I'm hurting,"
- "I can't do this alone."

There is no shame in that. In fact, there is great courage in speaking your truth.

The Role of Faith in Strength.

When our own strength runs out, God steps in. His strength is made perfect in our weakness. Sometimes, the strongest thing you can do is whisper, " God, carry me today.

"But those who hope in the Lord will renew their strength. They will soar on wings like eagles..."

-Isaiah 40: 31

CHAPTER 4:
WHEN HOPE FEELS FAR AWAY

There are moments when hope feels like a stranger – distant, unreachable, and silent. Days when getting out of bed feels impossible. Nights when the darkness wraps around you and won't let go. In these moments, it's easy to wonder if things will ever change.

The Weight of Waiting:

Waiting for healing – Whether physical, emotional, or spiritual, can be exhausting. It tests your Faith. It stretches your patience. And sometimes, it makes you question if God still hears you.

But waiting doesn't mean God is absent; sometimes he is working in the silence, preparing your heart, building something deeper in you.

"The darkest night often leads to the brightest morning."

TINY SPARKS OF HOPE:

Hope doesn't always come in big miracles. Sometimes, it shows up in small ways.

- A smile from someone who sees you.
- A song that touches your heart.

- A scripture that finds you right when you need it.

Hope is a quiet fighter. It doesn't give up, even when you feel like you have.

You Are Still Hare:

And that matters, no matter what yesterday looks like. That means your story isn't over. There's still time for healing, joy, and peace.

With God, all things are possible for those who believe. Be nlessed.

A Prayer for When Hope Feels Far Away.

Dear God,

When hope feels distant and my heart feels heavy, remind me that you are near. Even when I can't see the way forward, hold my hand.

Even when I feel like giving up, whisper that I'm not alone. Help me believe in healing, even when it's slow.

Help me trust in you, even if it's quiet. Thank you for never leaving me – not even for a moment

Amen.

Whisper in the Wilderness:

The silence that follows her prayer was not empty – it pulsed softly, like a quiet heartbeat beneath the soil. She sat there, knees down up, arms wrapped tightly around them, listening. Not for an answer, not even for comfort, but for the simple assurance that she was not alone in the ache.

Morning hadn't yet broken, but the sky hinted at it, blushing faintly behind the silhouetted trees. The coolness in the air kissed her cheeks, and for a brief moment, she imagined it was the breath of the Divine – gentle, not rushing her to heal, not pushing her to be strong, just present.

I'm still here, she whispered into the silence. It wasn't a declaration of strength, but of stubborn grace. The kind of grace that shows up barefoot in the dark, knees sore from kneeling, still believing that hope is worth waiting for.

She stood slowly, brushing leaves from her skirt, and stepped towards the narrow path that wove deeper into the trees. Each footfall felt deliberate, like a question asked in faith. The forest, still asleep in shadows, didn't answer. But it didn't resist her either. Sometimes, that was enough.

As she walked, memories surfaced like mist, soft, clinging, impossible to hold. The sound of her mother's voice singing hymns while stirring the soup. The way her father once held her hand in Church when the preacher spoke of Storms. And the journey, yes, the old journal tucked into her satchel, filled with promises she had once believed without question.

She paused and it out, the worn leather cover familiar beneath her finger. Flipping it open, she scanned the pagers until she reached the one that had nearly unraveled her:

"Even in the desert, my streams do not run dry."

She didn't feel like a stream. She felt like dust.

But she kept walking.

She came upon a clearing – a quiet circle of earth where the trees bowed just slightly, as if they too were weary from

Standing so long. In the center stood a stone, smooth and wide like a table prepared for something sacred.

She sat upon it, the journal still in hand, and looked up. The first sliver of sunlight pierced the canopy, landing across her face like a blessing.

It didn't erase the sorrow. But it warmed it. And somehow, that made it bearable.

She took a breath and wrote in the margin of the page, under the verse: " I am not stream. But I will wait by the river."

And with that, this chapter found its quiet ending, not in resolution, but in the choice to keep believing, even in between.

CHAPTER 5:
WHEN THE SILENCE SPEAKS

The days that followed passed not with thunder or miracle, but with small, almost forgettable moments – the hold the weight of survival. She rose with the sun and slept when the stars came. She boiled water over a fire built with trembling hands. She spoke aloud. Sometimes, just to hear her own voice. And slowly, the silence around her began to change.

It no longer felt like absence. It felt like waiting.

Waiting, not for a rescue, but for a revealing. There was something here in the stillness, in the ache, in the unanswered prayers – that was shaping her. Not into someone stronger, but someone truer.

One evening, she found herself tracking the lines of her palm, wondering if the story written there had always included this wilderness. She didn't have answers. But she had this moment, and it asked only for her honesty.

So she whispered:

"I don't know how to heal. But I want to."

And the wind stirred, like a breath of agreement. The next morning brought a soft rain – not the kind that floods, but the kind that hushes the world. She sat under the shatter of a leaning cedar, listening to the rhythm as it tapped leaves, stones, and skin alike.

She opened the journal again, its pages slightly warped now from mist and handling. She didn't write, not yet. She just held it. Sometimes presence was the prayer.

It was then she noticed the smallest thing, a green shoot pushing up beside her boot, rising bravely through the damp earth. Life, unbothered by her pain, but not mocking it either. Simple continuing.

She stared at it for a long time. And then, without thinking, she whispered, " Grow anyway."

She didn't know if she was talking to the shoot or herself. May both. Maybe it didn't matter.

Because the rain kept falling and the green kept rising.

That afternoon, she wandered further than usual, past the grove she'd claimed as her own and into unfamiliar wood. The trees here were older, taller, their bark thick with time. It felt like walking through a memory she hadn't lived.

Her steps slowed. Not from fear, but reverence. Something about this place made her heart quiet in a different way, as if the ground remembered prayers spoken centuries ago.

She found a fallen log and sat, letting her hands rest in her lap. She didn't plan to speak, but the words found her anyway.

"What if I'm never whole again"?

The breeze shifted, wrapping her in the scent of moss and pine. No answer came. Only the sense that the question was welcome and that even her doubts, her hands rested in her lap. She didn't plan to speak, but the words found her anyway.

CHAPTER 6:
THE FLAME THAT WOULDN'T DIE

The breeze shifted, wrapping her in the scent of moss and pine. No answer came, only the sense that the question was welcome – that even her doubts were allowed here.

She closed her eyes.

And in the dark behind her eyelids, she imagined a light not blinding or loud, but steady like a candle kept burning in a long–forgotten chapel.

It didn't promise a map.

But it promised it wouldn't go out.

That small flame, cradled in the hollow of her palm, danced with the wind but never surrendered to it. She moved forward, each step uncertain, but lit just enough to keep going. Shadows pressed in from all, fearful of the light she carried.

In the silence, her thoughts grew louder. Was she following something, or merely feeling what was behind? The path didn't answer, and the flame didn't care. It just burned. Quiet. Constant. Present.

She paused at the edge of the clearing, the trees bending slightly as if whispering secrets to one another.

The air felt heavier here, thick with expectation. Somewhere ahead, something was waiting. Not a threat – at least not yet – but a presence. Ancient. Watchful.

She tightened her grip around the flame, though it gave no heat, only light. "I'm still here", she whispered, unsure if it was to herself, the trees, or whatever might be listening. The flame flickered in response, not brighter, not dimmer, just awake.

The ground beneath her feet felt different now. Less like earth, more like memory. Each step pulled her deeper not just into the forest, but into herself. Into the things she had buried. Names. Faces. Regrets.

And still, the flame didn't go out.

The wind rose, fierce and sudden, curling through the branches like a warning. Leaves scattered at her feet, and the sky overhead rumbled with distant thunder. Still, she didn't turn back.

No matter how the storm is, she reminded herself, always believe you are walking with God. Have faith in Him.

And in the moment, the flame steadied, standing taller than before. It was as if the words themselves fed it, hope made visible. She took a breath, deeper than any in days, and stepped into the storm, not with fear, but with faith.

CHAPTER 7:
THE VOICE IN THE SILENCE

The storm passed, not with fury, but with grace – as though it had come only to test her heart, not break it. The air was crispy now, cleansed, and every drop clinging to the leaves shimmered like a quiet hallelujah. She walked in stillness, and the forest answered with its own silence, deep and ancient.

That was when she heard it. Not a sound exactly, but a stirring, like a whisper beneath her ribs. A presence, not outside of her, but within. Not loud. Not urgent. But steady. Kind. "My Child."

She stopped. The flame in her hand didn't flicker this time. It bowed, as if in reverence.

"I'm listening", she said softly.

And for the first time in a long time, she wasn't afraid of what might come next.

The voice didn't respond immediately. It simply held space, and in that at space, she began to understand. The questions that had been echoing in her heart – about her path, her purpose, the darkness – began to quiet, not because the answers arrived all at once, but because she realized she had been walking toward them all along.

"You have carried the flame well, but it's not just for you", the voice said, this time clearer as though it had been waiting for her, though agreeing."

She closed her eyes, feeling the weight of its warmth and cool air all around. She understood now that her journey was not one of survival, but one of sharing – of light, of hope, of faith.

"The world is heavy with darkness," the voice continued, "but the light within you is strong enough to bear it. You will not walk alone, but you must walk forward. Trust in what you cannot see, and in the promises you have not yet been given."

Her heart stirred, a mixture of awe and uncertainty. The weight of the task ahead seemed enormous, yet the flame in her hand grew brighter, and a quiet peace settled in her chest.

She took another step forward, and the whisper in her soul was now a guide. The path stretched out ahead, unknown, but she was ready.

For the first time, she wasn't just walking through the forest. She was walking with purpose.

She moved forward, the forest parting slightly to accommodate her. It was as if the trees themselves recognized her presence now, the air clearer, the ground more solid beneath her feet. She no longer felt lost, though the path ahead remained unseen, wrapped in shadows and uncertainty.

The flame in her hand grew brighter with each step. It cast long, soft shadows on the earth, not to repel the darkness, but to blend with it, showing that light could live alongside the dark without fear.

The voice came again, gentler now, like a breeze through the leaves.

"There are others who walk this path, to though they may not see yet. You will find them when the time is right.

She paused, her brow furrowing slightly. Other? She hadn't seen another soul in days, maybe weeks. Had they been following her? Or were they ahead?

Questions arise, but she pushed them aside for now. The flame was enough. The voice was enough. And if others were out there, she would find them when the time came.

As if in answer, the ground before her shifted. A soft glow rose from the earth, faint but distinct – a light not like the flame in her hand, but like a reflection of it far ahead.

She quickened her pace, the light growing brighter with each step. It was not the same as the light of her flame, but it called to her, a beacon that stirred something deep within her – something familiar, yet distant.

The trees began to thin, and the land opened up into a wide valley. In the distance, there was a stone archway, old and worn, but still standing. Beyond it, a shadow moved, slow, deliberate, and undeniably human.

She wasn't alone.

"You have not left them. You carry them within you. But you must walk this path alone, for now. The light within you is not just for them, it is for you, too."

She felt the weight of those words settle in her heart, and she understood. The path she walked wasn't about leaving her loved ones behind; it was about discovering a part of herself she had forgotten. It was not abandonment, it was a journey of becoming.

The figure in the distance was still there, but now she understood that the person she was meant to find wasn't just out there, waiting for her to catch up. It was the woman who carried the flame. The one standing right here, walking forward.

And she would find her way.

She stood still for a moment, letting the weight of the distance settle into her bones. The figure in the distance, her reflection, remained unmoving, as though caught in time. She knew she had to continue. The path ahead wasn't about reconciling with her past; it was about stepping into the unknown, where every step would either reveal more of herself, or force her to confront what she'd buried. With each step, the valley stretches further, and the light of the flame grows more distinct. But still, the figure in the distance didn't move. She thought of her family again – their voices calling her name, the gentle pull of their love, and the safety they once provided. She remembered the familiar faces at her place of worship, the sense of belonging that had once anchored her, grounding her with the love and faith they shared.

But now, those faces were blurry images in the back of her mind, fading into the distance like shadows at sunset.

"Why am I so far away from them"? She whispered, her voice trembling as she spoke the question aloud for the first time.

The wind swirled around her, carrying with it the voice she had come to trust.

"Not far," it replied, "You are closer to them than you know. The distance is an illusion. You carry them within you, within your heart, within your spirit. The path you walk is not one of separation, but of connection.

You will see them again, but first, you must find the light within yourself. The one they always saw in you."

Her grip on the flame tightened. There was comfort in those words, but also a quiet, unsettling truth. Could she truly walk this path without the safety net of her past? Could she leave behind the familiar and still hold onto the love they had shared?

She looked up at the figure once more. It was still there, unmoving. She wasn't close enough for her to walk past it. Perhaps it wasn't the destination that mattered, but the understanding of who she had become in the process.

As she walked closer to the archway, she realized that the landscape itself had begun to shift. The once–barren valley was now dotted with patches of green, small but growing, like new life taking root in the cracks of a stone wall. There was a subtle beauty in the transition, a reminder that even in the darkest places, life would always find a way.

Her thoughts were interrupted by a distant sound – a low hum that seemed to resonate from the earth itself. It was neither threatening nor comforting, but it stirred something deep within her.   She turned in the direction of the sound and saw the archway now glowing with a faint, golden light.

"She forward", the voice urged. "What you seek lies beyond this threshold. Your journey is not over, but you must move forward to truly see."

When she hesitated, she walked toward the arch, the hum growing louder with each step. As she passed beneath it, the world around her seemed to shift again – time itself felt like it was stretching, like the past and the future were both wrapped up in this single moment.

The figure that had once seemed so distant was now beside her. Her reflection. The woman she had once been, standing beside the woman she was becoming.

"You are not alone", the voice reminded her. "You never were."

And for the first time in what felt like forever, she believed it.

CHAPTER 8:
THE MORNING LIGHT

The morning light was softer than usual, spilling through the window like a quiet invitation. She lay still, listening – not just to the sound around her, but to the silence within her. It wasn't empty this time. It was calm

For the first time in a long time, she sat up without the weight pressing quite so hard on her chest. She reached for the mug on her nightstand, fingers brushing the chipped ceramic. It was cold, untouched from the night before, but today, she noticed it. That, in itself, felt like progress.

The voice, whether it was memory, imagination, or something more, still echoed gently in her mind. "You never were." The words didn't erase the pain, but they softened it, gave it shape. And with shape came the possibility of carrying it differently.

Outside, the world moves on: birdsong, a dog barking in the distance, footsteps on the pavement. Ordinary things. And somehow, they didn't feel so far away anymore.

A soft knock at the door startled her. She hesitated, heart fluttering not in fear, but in unfamiliar anticipation.

Another knock. Then a voice, low and careful. "Hey…
it's me. I brought you something."

She knew that voice. Even after weeks – maybe
months – of silence, it wrapped around her like a familiar
blanket. She rose, slowly, and padded to the door.

When she opened it, there he was. Ben was standing
with a paper bag in one hand, uncertainty in his eyes, and
warmth he didn't know he still carried.

"I didn't know if you'd be up," he said. "I wasn't ", she
replied, a small smile playing at the corners of her lips.
"But I am now."

They stood there for a moment, neither sure how to
begin. Then Ben held out the back.

"Still your favorite", he said. "Cinnamon rolls from
that little bakery on 6th. The one you used to swear healed
your soul."

She let out a breath – half laugh, half disbelief – as she
took the bag

"You remembered."

"I remember more than you think", he said quietly. "I
just didn't know if I was allowed to anymore."

Her eyes dropped to the bag, then back to him. "I don't
know what I'm allowed to anymore. But thank you."

He nodded, stepping just enough closer to that she could feel the warmth between them. Not touching, just…. There.

"I didn't come to fix anything", he said. "I just wanted you to know I never stopped thinking about you, even when you went quiet. Especially then."

She looks at him, eyes shimmering – not from tears, but from something deeper. "That's when I needed to be thought of the most", she whispered.

She stepped aside, opening the door a little wider. "Come in", she said. Unless you have somewhere else to be."

He shook his head. Nowhere more important than here."

They settled at a small kitchen table, worn at the edge, marked by years of hurried breakfasts and quiet evenings. She opened the bag, the scent of cinnamon and warm sugar curling into the room.

He watched her take a bite, the first real food she'd tasted in what felt like days. Weeks, maybe, she closed her eyes for a second, just long enough to remember what comfort used to feel like.

"You always had a thing for cinnamon", he said, smiling. " Said it reminded you of your Mom's Kitchen."

She nodded. "She used to bake when things got hard. Not for anyone else. Just for herself. I guess I picked that up."

He tore a piece of his roll and glanced around. "I missed this place. It still feels like you. Even with the dust."

She laughed softly. "Yeah, I haven't exactly been hosting guests."

"I didn't come as a guest", he said gently. "I came because I couldn't stay away any longer."

"I'm glad", she said finally. "Even if I don't know what to do with it yet ".

"You don't have to do anything", he replied. "We can just sit here. Eat cinnamon rolls and talk or not "?

She met his eyes. "Let's talk. There's too piece. Even the broken ones." She met his eyes. "Let's talk. There's too much I kept inside. Too much, I thought no one would want to hear.

"I want to hear all of it", Ben said. "Every piece. Even the broken one."

He took a slow breath, fingers tracing the rim of his coffee mug. "But.... Maybe I should start first."

She looked at him, surprised. "You"?

He nodded, eyes steady. "Yeah, I've been carrying something, too."

The room quieted around them, no longer heavy, just still, holding space.

"I was scared", he began. "Back when you started pulling away.... I told myself to give you space. That maybe you'd come back when you were ready. But the truth is, I was afraid I'd say the wrong thing. Or not say enough. So I said nothing."

She didn't interrupt, didn't flinch. Just listened.

"I thought I was helping by staying back. But I wasn't. I was just... about", he said, voice low. "And I hated myself for it."

Her expression softened. "Ben, I never needed you to fix it. I just needed to know someone was there."

"I know that now", he said. "But back then, I didn't know how to be there without trying to make it better. And when I couldn't, it was useless."

"You weren't", she whispered.

Their eyes held for a long moment. No blame. Just truth.

The silence between them wasn't awkward – it was meaningful. Full of everything they hadn't said before, but now had the courage to face.

She reached across the table, her fingers brushing crumbs as they moved toward his hand. Slowly, carefully, she placed her hand over his.

It was warm. Steady. Real.

Ben stilled. Not because he was surprised, but because he didn't want to move too fast, didn't want to break whatever had just settled between them.

She gave his hand the lightest squeeze. " You're here now. That matters more than anything you didn't do."

He turned his hand over so their palms touched, fingers folding around hers. Not tight. Just sure.

And for a moment, that was enough. No fixing. No fear. Just cinnamon sweet air, two hands resting together, and the quiet beginning of something mending.

CHAPTER 9:
THE MORNING LIGHT SPILLED SOFTLY

The morning light spilled softly through the blinds, painting the floor in quiet stripes of gold. It was the kind of light that asked nothing, neither action nor answer – only presence.

She stirred slowly, as if the world would wait. For once, it did. Outside, the street murmured its usual song: distant traffic, a dog barking, the occasional flutter of wings against the windowpane. But inside, everything felt paused – held in the warm hush left by the night before.

There was still so much undone, still so much unknown. But its weight didn't press quite so hard now. Not with the scent of cinnamon still lingering faintly in the air. Not with the memory of two hands – hesitant, Steady, resting together like a promise neither of them dared to speak aloud yet.

She let herself breathe into the moment. Not the future. Not the past. Just now.

She stood at the kitchen counter, absently tracing the rim of her mug. The tea had long gone cold, but she hadn't noticed. Her thoughts were far from the ceramic warmth and drifting somewhere between memory and maybe.

The silence was different now. Not empty, but expectant, like the moment just before a sea breaks open underground. Something had shifted.

The door creaked slightly as he stepped in. No sudden movements, no heavy footsteps, just a quiet presence, unsure but willing. Their eyes met briefly. Neither looked away.

"Morning", he said, his voice still rough with sleep.

She nodded. " Morning."

It wasn't dramatic. No declaration. No sweeping changes. But in that small exchange lived a world of possibility. Trust wasn't rebuilt overnight, but maybe – just maybe – it had begun.

He moved to the stove, reaching for the kettle. "Want me to warm that up for you?"

A pause. A breath.

"You", she said. "Thanks."

It was nothing. It was everything.

Later that afternoon, she found herself in the old bookstore on 5th and Maple – the one with the crooked shelves and the bell over the door that never rang quite right. It had always been her retreat, her quiet rebellion against a world that moved too fast.

The air inside smelled like sun–warmed paper and dust, comforting and familiar. She ran her fingers along the spines as she walked, letting instincts guide her rather than title or cover.

In the back corner, nestled between a forgotten poetry section and a stack of used journals, she spotted it: a weathered copy of letters to a young poet. She pulled it free, the pages soft with age, the words waiting like old friends.

A low voice interrupted her reverie.

"I didn't think anyone else still read Rilke", he said.

She turned to find a stranger, thirties, glasses sliding down his nose, holding a leather–bound notebook. There was something open in his face. Not forward. Just curious.

"I do", she replied, tucking the book under her arm. "Especially when I forget how to listen to myself."

He nodded, thoughtful. "Same."

They stood in silence, not uncomfortable, just suspended in a moment that didn't need to be filled. Then he smiled – not a big one, just a flicker – and stepped back.

"Good choice," he said, and disappeared into the aisles.

She stood there for a moment longer, the book pressed against her chest. And somewhere deep inside, something steady stirred.

She paid for the book with a few crumpled bills, the cashier barely glancing up as the bell clanged out its lopsided farewell. Outside, the sky was heavy with the kind of clouds that don't threaten rain, just introspection.

As she walked home, letters to a Young Poet tucked safely in her bag, she kept thinking about the stranger – not because of anything extraordinary he'd done, but because of how ordinary it had felt. Easy undemanding.

And in a life that had been anything but, that meant something.

She didn't even know his Name. Not yet.

The apartment greeted her with the familiar hush of absence. No music, no voices. Just the soft creak of floorboards as she moved through the space.

She set the book gently on the coffee table, next to the mug she hadn't finished that morning. The scent of cinnamon was long gone now, but she remembered it all the same, how it had wrapped around them like a blanket, how it had made the silence feel less lonely.

He was in the next room, door slightly ajar. She could hear the faint rustle of paper, the occasional sigh. There was a time not long ago when she'd have ignored it. Or resented it. But now, it just sounded human.

She reached for the blanket draped over the couch and curled into the corner, pulling her knees up. Her fingers found the edge of letters to a Young Poet and opened it without thinking.

Halfway down the page, Alvin wrote: "Be patient toward all that is unsolved in your heart and try to love the questions themselves…"

She read the line again, slower this time. It felt like something she hadn't known she needed to hear. Like a light left on in a distant room.

The door creaked softly, and he stepped out – hair tousled, a paper in his hand.

"Hey," he said quieter this time. "I found something you might want to see."

She looked up, blinking out of the book and into his face. There was something different there. Not entirely new, just less guarded.

"Okay," she said, unfolding herself from the couch. "Show me."

She followed him down the hall, the quiet stretching comfortably between them.

Whatever he had to show her could wait. For now, it was enough to walk beside him, the air still holding a trace of something unspoken. The kind of silence that doesn't demand explanation, only presence.

And as they turned the corner, disappearing into the soft shadows of the room beyond, she felt something settle.

Not closure.

But the beginning of trust is unfolding – page by page.

CHAPTER 10:
THE ROOM WAS DIM

The room was dim, lit only by the soft spill of late afternoon sun filtering through the sheer curtains. Dust floated in the light like slow-moving fireflies, and the air held that peculiar stillness just before something changes.

He handed her the paper without a word.

She took it, careful not to smudge the edges. It wasn't much; it was just a single sheet torn from a notebook, the handwriting uneven, and a little rushed. Her eyes scanned it quickly, then again, slower this time. It was a list.

A list of things he remembered. About her

The pink sweater was what she always wore when it rained. The way she hummed when she peeled oranges. How she always reads the last page of a book first. The way she looked up when she was trying not to cry. The cinnamon.

His breath caught somewhere between her ribs.

He stood there, not asking anything of her, not explaining. Just letting the moment exist, bare and real.

She folded the paper carefully, like something fragile. Sacred.

"I didn't know you noticed", she whispered.

"I didn't think I did", he said. "Until I started writing it down."

They didn't speak for a while after that; there was nothing to add, and nothing to fix. Just a quiet acknowledgement between two people learning how to see each other again.

The next day, she returned to the bookstore – not searching, just drawn.

The bell above the door stammered out its usual crooked greeting, and the familiar scent wrapped around her like a worn coat. She wasn't sure what she was looking for. Maybe nothing. Maybe space.

She wandered past the new releases and past the cookbooks with glossy covers, trailing her fingers along the shelves until she found herself back near poetry, where the spines leaned like tired shoulders. And there he was again. The stranger.

This time, seated on a stool, scribbling in the same leather-bound notebook.

He looked up just as she turned the corner, and recognition passed between them like a quiet signal – no surprise, no awkwardness. Just a nod, and something warmer.

"I wondered if you'd come back", he said.

She arched an eyebrow. "I wasn't planning to."

He smiled, soft and sideways. "Neither was I."

There was a pause, comfortable again.

"I never got your name," she said.

"Louis," he offered, holding out a hand. "You?"

She took it. "Alice."

His handshake was firm but brief, just enough. "Well, Alice," he said, since we're both here not planning to... maybe fate's being a little pushy." She laughed – quiet and unguarded. "Maybe."

Louis glanced down at the notebook. "I jot things down here. Observation. Lines that don't go anywhere. Want to hear one?"

She hesitated, then nodded.

He flipped to a page near the middle and read:

"Some people walk in like punctuation. Others – like the beginning of a sentence you didn't know you were writing."

Alice didn't respond right away. The words settled somewhere deep.

"I like that." She said at last. "It feels... honest."

Louis closed the notebook with a quiet snap. "That's rare praise."

She tilted her head. "You might get used to it."

As she stepped back out into the fading light, Alice felt the late spring breeze press against her skin – cool, gentle, alive.

The sidewalk was the same. The noise, the rhythm of the city, it hadn't changed. But something inside her had.

She walked slowly, one hand in her pocket, the other resting on the spine of letters to a Young Poet inside her bag. Louis's words echoed safety in her mind. Not loud. Not urgent. Just....there.

A sentence she didn't know she had started writing.

She didn't know what it meant yet. She didn't have to.

For the first time in a long time, not knowing didn't feel like a threat. It felt like possibility.

CHAPTER 11:
PARALLEL MOMENT

The rain had been steady for hours, soft as breath, but insistent. It tapped against Alice's windowpane like a question she didn't know how to answer. Inside, the apartment was dim, lit only by the yellow spill of a small lamp and the muted glow of the piano keys. She sat there barefoot, in an oversized sweater, her fingers resting on the keys like they were sleeping limbs.

She played a single note.

Then another.

A half-melody, then nothing. Silence stretched, long and fragile.

The piano had always been a place she escaped to – or maybe hid behind. But tonight, it felt like standing in front of a mirror she couldn't quite look into. Each note she played felt like it echoed too deeply inside her. It wasn't just about Louis. It was about the long years of holding herself together so tightly she forgot what softness felt like.

She pressed a chord that trembled – minor, unresolved – and let it hang in the air.

Across the city, on the rooftop of a building that had seen better days, Louis stood still under the small overhang. His coat was damp at the edges, but he didn't mind. The rain brought a kind of stillness he hadn't felt in weeks. In the hush of it, he could almost believe the noise in his mind was just part of the weather.

He lit a cigarette, more for the ritual than the smoke. The tip glowed, then faded, then glowed again. He didn't inhale deeply. He just watched the curl of smoke drift up and away – like a thought he wasn't ready to keep.

His phone buzzed in his pocket. He didn't reach for it.

He was thinking about Alice. About the way her eyes looked when she wasn't guarding them, about the things he almost said, and the things he never dared to.

They were so different. And yet – maybe not. Maybe just scarred in different shapes.

Back at the piano, Alice exhaled and stood. She walked to the window and leaned her forehead against the cool glass. She watched the streetlights blur through the water, the way the city seemed soft and distorted, like everything was a little too tender to face directly.

She picked up her phone and opened a message draft.

"I don't know what I'm doing, but keep thinking about the way you looked at me – not like you saw someone broken, but like you weren't afraid of the cracks."

She stared at it. Her thumb hovered. Then she signed and deleted it.

On the rooftop, Louis pulled his phone out and typed slowly, deliberately.

"If I knew how to fix myself, I would've done it already. But maybe I don't need to be fixed. Maybe I just need someone who doesn't flinch when it gets dark."

He read it twice. Then hit backspace until the screen was blank.

They didn't send the messages. But they had written them. And maybe that was something.

In their separate spaces, with the rain between them, Alice and Louis each stood still – hearts half–open, half afraid.

The city hummed below. The night went on.

And somewhere in the quiet, something inside both of them shifted – not loud, not obvious, but real.

Scene 1: Alice – The Piano

Rain tapped at the windows like a memory trying to return. Alice sat at the piano in her dim apartment, the glow of the desk lamp casting shadows across the keys. Her fingers hovered, uncertain.

She played two notes – hesitant, soft.

The Silence.

She closed her eyes, trying to find something inside herself that music might reach. But all she found was the arch that had followed her for weeks now. Not sharp, not loud. Just constant – like a bruise that never stopped pulsing.

She played again. A minor chord. Unfinished. Like her.

Her hand trembled. She stopped.

The silence filled the room again. Thick and almost kind.

Scene 2: Louis – Rooftop

Louis leaned on the rooftop railing, eyes on the city below. The rain was light here, just enough to bead on his coat and blur the glow of passing traffic.

He hadn't planned to come up here, but his apartment felt too loud, too small. Up here, the world breathed wider.

He pulled out a cigarette. Lit it. Let the smoke drift slowly from his lips. He didn't even want it. It just gave his hands something to do.

He thought about Alice.

About how she looked when she didn't know he was watching – thoughtful, a little worn at the edges. Honest in a way that frightened him. Not because of her pain – but because he saw pieces of himself in it.

He hadn't told her that part.

Maybe he never would.

Scene 3: Alice – The window

Alice rose from the piano and walked to the window. The city below shimmered, blurred through the droplets. She pressed her forehead to the glass, letting the cold anchor her. Falling apart in their hands?

She opened her phone. Her fingers typed before she had time to think.

She stared at the windows.

Then deleted them.

She set the phone down and let herself cry. Quietly. Rain against glass.

Scene 4: Louis – The Unsent Message

Louis's phone buzzed. He ignored it. Instead, he opened a new message, thumb hovering.

He stared at the screen for a long time. Then backspaced it into nothing.

The cigarette burned low. He flicked the ash into the wind

Somewhere out there, she was feeling something he couldn't name. And maybe that was enough – for now.

He tucked the phone away and looked out over the city again. Not searching. Just staying.

Closing Beat

Later that night, in two different places, they both reached for sleep but didn't quiet find it.

Alice lay on her side, the pillow damp, the piano keys still echoing in her mind. Louis sat on the edge of his bed, shoes still on, staring at nothing and everything.

Neither knew the other had almost reached out.

But in the spaces between silence and rain, something had begun to shift, a thread tightening, however softly, between two quiet hearts.

CHAPTER 12:
THE FIRST LIGHT

The café was almost empty – just the quiet scrape of chairs, the low clink of cups being set down, and the steady hum of something warm beginning.

Alice stood outside for a long minute before pushing the door open. She almost turned away twice. Her hands were cold inside her coat pockets, her breath visible in the morning chill. But she walked in anyway.

Inside, the light was soft – the kind that forgives.

Louis was already there. Seated at a corner table, black coffee in front of him, fingers laced loosely together. He looked up as she approached, and something in his face didn't flinch.

"He," she said, her voice small but steady.

"Hey," he replied. "I didn't know if you'd come."

"I didn't cither."

A pause. Not awkward. Just careful.

Alice sat across from him. The table between them felt smaller than she expected. She looked at his hands, then at the window beside them, where the light was beginning to spill onto the street.

"I'm not here to explain anything," she said finally. "I don't have answers. I just.... I don't want the silence to be the last thing."

Louis nodded slowly. "Me neither."

They didn't smile. Not yet. But there was something in the air – a loosening. A letting in.

"I keep thinking," he began, "that we're supposed to get better before we let someone see us. But maybe... maybe we don't have to wait. Maybe we just show up. As is."

Alice looked at him, eyes tired but clear. "And hope that's enough?"

"And keep showing up," he said. " Even when it's not easy."

Outside, a dog barked somewhere down the street. A bus passed. The world went on.

They sat there, not reaching across the table, but not pulling away either. Two people not fixed, not whole – but present. And for now, that was everything.

A small, almost invisible smile pulled at the corner of Alice's mouth. She looked out the window again.

"*Light's changing," she said.*

Louis followed her gaze. "Yeah. It is."

And in the quiet that followed, something opened. Not loudly. Not all at once.

Just enough.

It's a beautiful ending: not about solving pain, but about choosing to stay in it together, which feels honest and true.